O Come Let Us Adore Him

Dennis L. Newman

DEDICATED TO

Shaaron Leigh Newman

the joy of my life,
my beautiful and loving wife of 54 years,
who loves and serves Jesus every day.
Her love of Christmas fills our home
with the sights, sounds and flavors of the season,
and with great anticipation, she looks forward to
celebrating with family and friends.
Her loving touch and attention to detail truly make it
the most joyous and meaningful time of year.
I love you sweetheart.

Trilogy Christian Publishers
A Wholly Owned Subsidiary of Trinity Broadcasting Network
2442 Michelle Drive, Tustin, CA 92780

Copyright © 2020 by Dennis L. Newman

Scripture quotations marked (KJV) taken from The Holy Bible, King James Version. Cambridge Edition: 1769.

For information, address Trilogy Christian Publishing Rights Department, 2442 Michelle Drive, Tustin, Ca 92780.

Trilogy Christian Publishing/ TBN and colophon are trademarks of Trinity Broadcasting Network.

For information about special discounts for bulk purchases, please contact Trilogy Christian Publishing.

Manufactured in the United States of America

Trilogy Disclaimer: The views and content expressed in this book are those of the author and may not necessarily reflect the views and doctrine of Trilogy Christian Publishing or the Trinity Broadcasting Network.

10 9 8 7 6 5 4 3 2 1

Library of Congress Cataloging-in-Publication Data is available.

ISBN 978-1-64773-520-3

ISBN 978-1-64773-521-0 (ebook)

O Come Let Us Adore Him

I want to salute my friend and fellow Christian, Dennis Newman, for providing more than a sample collection of Christmas carols. Not only is this selection rich in tradition but beautiful in its presentation.

I can foresee this collection of beloved carols being in every home, adding to the traditions of putting up a tree and hanging stockings.

May those who discover this gift rejoice in the love and peace the season brings.

Additional for pastors/leaders:

As a pastor, I believe it would be worthy for church leaders to offer copies of this song book to those in their congregations, as a way of revisiting a great tradition of joy and the wonder of the Savior's birth.

Pastor Jack W. Hayford
Founding Pastor, The Church On The Way, Van Nuys, CA
Founder and Chancellor Emeritus, The King's University, Dallas, TX

Oh, give thanks to the Lord, for He is good!
For His mercy endures forever.
Psalm 118:29 (NKJV)

I love Christmas. In fact, I am passionate about Christmas. The reality of Divinity coming to earth in order that mankind might be reconciled with Father God is the Best News there is. A couple of decades ago, I originated a programming theme for The Family Channel which became known as "25 Days of Christmas," the most successful block of programming in the history of the network which has continued to this day on the channel's successor networks. The head of programming called me "Father Christmas," a name I was always happy to embrace. My dear friend, Dennis Newman, shares my passion for Christmas. Following the leading of the Spirit over a ten year period, he has crafted a beautiful Christmas songbook which will certainly be a blessing to all who take the time to meditate on these timeless words—words that speak to the birthing of God's life and purposes in us, words of hope which bring light into our being.

Larry "Father Christmas" Dantzler
Board of Trustees, The King's University and Seminary

Having been a guest in the home of Dennis and Shaaron Newman on frequent occasions, it is of no surprise that the meticulous planning that goes into our visits is reflected in the production of this Christmas Carol and song book: the design, the touching tribute that Dennis gives to his wife Shaaron, the artwork and the succinct synopsis at the beginning of each carol—all of this is so beautifully produced.

As a retired pastor from the UK, I look back over many years of ministry and what has always been a cause of concern for me is what one writer has called "worship wars." Do we sing the old hymns/songs or the new ones? As a lover of both, I have no axe to grind. When it comes to Carols, the people of God are by and large united. They love them all. And here in this book, there is a mixture of both old and new. The test of any song, whether ancient or modern, is in its content and here in these carols you have theology set to music. What a delightful expression this book is of our praise to God.

Rev. Trevor Partington
Elim, United Kingdom
Chairman of Stafford Street Pastors

Foreword

There are many religious traditions that in one form or another celebrate milestones or major events related to their beliefs. Muslims celebrate Eid Al-Fitr, which is a celebratory day of feasting that ends their annual month of Ramadan (a month of fasting for Muslims during the day). Hindus participate annually in a celebratory festival called Diwali, the Festival of Lights. And the Jewish culture, of course, celebrates Hanukkah; eight nights of giving and receiving gifts as they reflect on the religious significance of the rededication of the second Jewish Temple, a very sacred place in Jewish tradition, in Jerusalem in 160 BC.

The Christmas celebration, however, is unique to all other religions in that followers of Jesus Christ around the globe celebrate the very birth of a Savior, Jesus Christ, who came to earth to become a living sacrifice for the sins of humanity. Of this Christ, even the famed emperor Napoleon Bonaparte declared, "Everything in Christ astonishes me! Neither history, nor humanity, nor the ages, nor nature, offer me anything with which I am able to compare Him and by which I am able to explain Him. In Him is everything extraordinary."

It is this Jesus that we celebrate at Christmas time. He was not just a good teacher, or even some profound religious prophet. He was the very Son of the Living God! So profound was Christ's entry upon earth (and so historically significant) that even our very calendars recognize year one as "the year of our Lord" (from the Latin Anno Domini, or more simply, AD). For Christians, the Christmas season is a time to recognize and celebrate the coming of our Savior to live among humankind, serve and suffer with them, and ultimately lay down His life for them, only to be gloriously resurrected in three days so those who believe in Him might have eternal life.

Annually for years Dennis and Shaaron Newman have kept this wonderful Christmas tradition alive by inviting loved ones, friends and neighbors at Christmas time to "come and adore" the true "reason for the season," our Lord and Savior, Jesus

Christ. Over the years they have compiled numerous of the most revered carols and Christmas hymns along with popular songs of the season to guide these times of adoration and fellowship around the warmth of a welcoming fireplace. *O Come Let us Adore Him* is the result. My wife Dee and I have been wonderfully encouraged to have experienced one of these occasions of blessing. So many friends have requested copies of this compilation that the Newman's felt it might be meaningful to make it available to a larger audience of those who feel as they do, that we need to keep this tradition alive now more than ever.

Even just reading (or singing) through these pages, and worshiping the Lord devotionally, will keep this season alive in your heart. Then, see if in the future you might want to invite friends, loved ones and neighbors at Christmas time to celebrate Jesus and the wonderful Christmas season together. It could well be an occasion of leading some of those precious friends or even loved ones who may not know Christ personally to experience the joy you have come to know in serving Him.

Dick Eastman
International President,
Every Home for Christ
(And President of America's
National Prayer Committee)

Acknowledgments

This book is the culmination of years of enjoying Christmas carols and songs around the piano at our home. Family and friends—young and old—all joyously singing about our Savior's birth, and enjoying the sights and sounds of the season.

It was one of these such occasions that prompted me to develop this lovely book of lyrics to our favorite songs. Thank you to Jeff and Cecilia Freeman who helped get the project started, and for their wonderful attention to all the details; from the choosing of songs to the writing and editing of content. Thank you Jeff for the years of leading our guests in worship and song at the piano—your infectious laugh and over-flowing joy ushered us into the Christmas Spirit.

Special thanks to Michelle Glush for her gifted design and thoughtful creation of this festive and beautiful book. Her love of Christmas and music is reflected in every page. I am grateful for her diligence and hard work not only in putting this book together, but also for her work with the printers and publisher, and other various tasks that have brought this book to fruition.

But most of all—all honor, glory and praise go to our Lord and Savior Jesus Christ —the baby who came at Bethlehem, and our Resurrected Messiah! You truly are our Wonderful, Counselor, Prince of Peace, and the soon and coming King.

Dennis Newman

Merry Christmas!

Christmas Greetings!

It truly is "the most wonderful time of the year" and we are so thankful you've decided to celebrate the birth of our Savior, Jesus Christ—the Light of the World!

Over a hundred years ago, folks would gather in homes to sing Christmas carols and rejoice in the magnificence of the season.

Reviving a lost tradition, we invite you to take a moment, put everything aside, and enter into this Christmas time with childlike excitement and expectancy as we enter the season with singing.

Enjoy the holidays with a profound sense of the Father's love for you. The Incarnation of God's love into a little baby who changed the course of the world is certainly reason for celebrating. Let's do it joyfully!

May this collection of Christmas carols and songs
inspire you to gather family, friends and neighbors together
to celebrate
The true meaning of Christmas—Jesus.

Dennis and Shaaron Newman

For unto us a Child is born, Unto us a Son is given;
And the government will be upon His shoulder.
And His name will be called Wonderful, Counselor, Mighty God,
Everlasting Father, Prince of Peace.
Isaiah 9:6 (NKJV)

Unto Us a Child is Born

Now there were in the same country shepherds
living out in the fields, keeping watch over their flock by night.
And behold, an angel of the Lord stood before them,
and the glory of the Lord shone around them,
and they were greatly afraid.

Then the angel said to them,
"Do not be afraid, for behold, I bring you
good tidings of great joy which will be to all people.
For there is born to you this day in the city of David
a Savior, who is Christ the Lord.
And this will be the sign to you:
You will find a Babe wrapped in swaddling cloths,
lying in a manger."

And suddenly there was with the angel a multitude
of the heavenly host praising God and saying:
"Glory to God in the highest,
And on earth peace, goodwill toward men!"
Luke 2:8-14 (NKJV)

Song List

Song List

Angels From The Realms Of Glory

First performed by Bob Hope and Marilyn Maxwell in
the motion picture, *The Lemon Drop Kid*, filmed in
July–August 1950 and released in March 1951.

Angels From The Realms Of Glory

Angels from the realms of glory,
Wing your flight o'er all the earth;
Ye who sang creation's story,
Now proclaim Messiah's birth:
Come and worship, come and worship,
Worship Christ, the newborn King!

Shepherds, in the fields abiding,
Watching o'er your flocks by night,
God with man is now residing,
Yonder shines the infant Light;
Come and worship, come and worship,
Worship Christ, the newborn King!

Sages, leave your contemplations,
Brighter visions beam afar;
Seek the great desire of nations,
Ye have seen His natal star;
Come and worship, come and worship,
Worship Christ, the newborn King!

Saints before the altar bending,
Watching long in hope and fear,
Suddenly the Lord, descending,
In His temple shall appear:
Come and worship, come and worship,
Worship Christ, the newborn King!

Angels We Have Heard On High

Written by Scottish poet James Montgomery, It was first printed in the Sheffield Iris on Christmas Eve 1816, although it only began to be sung in churches after its 1825 reprinting in the Montgomery collection.

Angels We Have Heard On High

Angels we have heard on high
Sweetly singing o'er the plains
And the mountains in reply
Echoing their joyous strains

Gloria in excelsis Deo
(Gloria in excelsis Deo)

Shepherds, why this jubilee?
Why your joyous strains prolong?
Say what may the tidings be
Which inspire your heav'nly song?

Come to Bethlehem and see
Him whose birth the angels sing
Come adore on bended knee
Christ the Lord, the newborn King

See within a manger laid
Jesus, Lord of heav'n and earth
Mary, Joseph, lend your aid
With us sing our Savior's birth

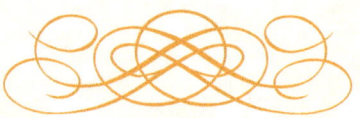

Away In A Manger

Originally thought to be the work of German religious reformer Martin Luther, the carol is now thought to be wholly American in creation. The two most-common musical settings are by William J. Kirkpatrick (1895) and James Ramsey Murray (1887).

Away In A Manger

Away in a manger, no crib for a bed,
The little Lord Jesus laid down His sweet head.
The stars in the sky looked down where He lay,
The little Lord Jesus asleep in the hay.

The cattle are lowing, the baby awakes,
But little Lord Jesus no crying He makes.
I love Thee, Lord Jesus, look down from the sky
And stay by my cradle till morning is nigh.

Be near me, Lord Jesus, I ask Thee to stay
Close by me forever, and love me, I pray.
Bless all the dear children in Thy tender care,
And take us to heaven, to live with Thee there.

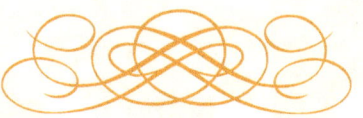

Deck The Halls

A traditional Christmas, yuletide, and New Year's carol.
The Welsh melody dates back to the sixteenth century.
The English lyrics, written by the Scottish musician
Thomas Oliphant, date back to 1862.

Deck The Halls

Deck the halls with boughs of holly
Fa la la la la la la la la
'Tis the season to be jolly
Fa la la la la la la la la
Don we now our gay apparel
Fa la la la la la la la la
Troll the ancient yuletide carol
Fa la la la la la la la la

See the blazing yule before us
Fa la la la la la la la la
Strike the harp and join the chorus
Fa la la la la la la la la
Follow me in merry measure
Fa la la la la la la la la
While I tell of yuletide treasure
Fa la la la la la la la la

Fast away the old year passes
Fa la la la la la la la la
Hail the new ye lads and lasses
Fa la la la la la la la la
Sing we joyous all together
Fa la la la la la la la la
Heedless of the wind and weather
Fa la la la la la la la la

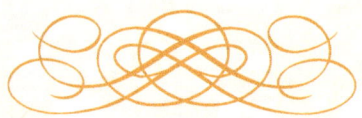

The First Noel

A traditional classical English Christmas carol of Cornish origin. Its current form was first published in *Carols Ancient and Modern* (1823) and *Gilbert and Sandys Carols* (1833), by William Sandys and Davies Gilbert.

The First Noel

The first Noel the angel did say
Was to certain poor shepherds in fields as they lay
In fields where they lay keeping their sheep
On a cold winter's night that was so deep

Noel, Noel, Noel, Noel
Born is the King of Israel

They looked up and saw a star
Shining in the east beyond them far
And to the earth it gave great light
And so it continued both day and night

And by the light of that same star
Three wise men came from country far
To seek for a king was their intent
And to follow the star wherever it went

Then let us all with one accord
Sing praises to our heavenly Lord
Who hath made heaven and earth of naught
And with His blood mankind hath bought

God Rest Ye Merry Gentlemen

An English traditional Christmas carol, dating back
to the 16th century or earlier. It is referred to in
Charles Dickens' *A Christmas Carol*, 1843.

God Rest Ye Merry Gentlemen

God rest ye merry gentlemen
Let nothing you dismay
Remember Christ our Savior
Was born on Christmas Day
To save us all from Satan's pow'r
When we were gone astray

O tidings of comfort and joy
Comfort and joy
O tidings of comfort and joy

And when they came to Bethlehem
Where our dear Savior lay
They found Him in a manger
Where oxen feed on hay
His mother Mary kneeling down
Unto the Lord did pray

Now to the Lord sing praises
All you within this place
And with true love and brotherhood
Each other now embrace
This holy tide of Christmas
All others doth deface

Go Tell It On The Mountain

An African-American spiritual song, compiled by
John Wesley Work, Jr., dating back to at least 1865. It has been
sung and recorded by many gospel and secular performers
and is considered a Christmas carol because
its original lyrics celebrate the Nativity of Jesus.

Go Tell It On The Mountain

Go tell it on the mountain
Over the hills and ev'rywhere
Go tell it on the mountain
That Jesus Christ is born

While shepherds kept their watching
O'er silent flocks by night
Behold throughout the heavens
There shone a holy light

The shepherds feared and trembled
When lo above the earth
Rang out the angel chorus
That hailed the Savior's birth

Down in a lowly manger
The humble Christ was born
And God sent us salvation
That blessed Christmas morn

13

Hark! The Herald Angels Sing

A Christmas carol that first appeared in 1739 in the collection *Hymns and Sacred Poems* with lyrics written by Charles Wesley. Wesley had requested and received slow and solemn music for his lyrics. The popular version is the result of alterations by various hands, notably by Wesley's co-worker George Whitefield who changed the opening couplet to the familiar one, and by Felix Mendelssohn, who wrote the melody.

Hark! The Herald Angels Sing

Hark, the herald angels sing
"Glory to the newborn King
Peace on earth and mercy mild
God and sinners reconciled!"
Joyful, all ye nations rise
Join the triumph of the skies
With th'angelic host proclaim
"Christ is born in Bethlehem!"
Hark, the herald angels sing, "Glory to the newborn King!"

Christ by highest heav'n adored
Christ the everlasting Lord
Late in time behold Him come
Offspring of the Virgin's womb
Veiled in flesh the Godhead see
Hail th'incarnate Deity
Pleased as man with men to dwell
Jesus, our Emmanuel
Hark, the herald angels sing, "Glory to the newborn King!"

Hail, the heav'n-born Prince of Peace
Hail, the Sun of Righteousness
Light and life to all He brings
Ris'n with healing in His wings
Mild He lays His glory by
Born that man no more may die
Born to raise the sons of earth
Born to give them second birth
Hark, the herald angels sing, "Glory to the newborn King!"

15

I Heard The Bells On Christmas Day

Based on the 1863 poem "Christmas Bells" by American poet Henry Wadsworth Longfellow. The carol was written during the American Civil War era and offered the renewed hope for peace on earth and good will toward men.

I Heard The Bells On Christmas Day

I heard the bells on Christmas Day
Their old familiar carols play,
And wild and sweet the words repeat
Of peace on earth, good will to men!

I thought how, as the day had come,
The belfries of all Christendom
Had rolled along the unbroken song
Of peace on earth, good will to men!

Till ringing, singing on its way,
The world revolved from night to day,
A voice, a chime, a chant sublime,
Of peace on earth, good will to men!

And in despair I bowed my head:
"There is no peace on earth," I said,
"For hate is strong and mocks the song
Of peace on earth, good will to men!"

Then pealed the bells more loud and deep:
"God is not dead, nor doth He sleep;
The wrong shall fail, the right prevail,
With peace on earth, good will to men!"

It Came Upon The Midnight Clear

A poem and Christmas carol written by
Edmund Sears, pastor of the Unitarian Church in
Wayland. It first appeared on December 29, 1849,
in the *Christian Register* in Boston.

It Came Upon The Midnight Clear

It came upon the midnight clear
That glorious song of old
From angels bending near the earth
To touch their harps of gold
"Peace on the earth, good will to men
From heaven's all gracious King!"
The world in solemn stillness lay
To hear the angels sing

And ye beneath life's crushing load
Whose forms are bending low
Who toil along the climbing way
With painful steps and slow
Look now for glad and golden hours
Come swiftly on the wing
O rest beside the weary road
And hear the angels sing

For lo, the days are hastening on
By prophet bards foretold
When with the ever-circling years
Comes round the age of gold
When peace shall over all the earth
Its ancient splendors fling
And the whole world give back the song
Which now the angels sing

19

Jingle Bells

One of the best-known American songs in the world. It was written by James Lord Pierpont (1822–1893) and published under the title "*One Horse Open Sleigh*" in the autumn of 1857. Originally intended for the Thanksgiving season, and having no connection to Christmas, it became associated with Christmas music decades after it was first performed in Boston in 1857.

Jingle Bells

Dashing through the snow
In a one-horse open sleigh
O'er the fields we go
Laughing all the way
Bells on bobtails ring
Making spirits bright
What fun it is to ride and sing
A sleighing song tonight

Jingle bells, jingle bells
Jingle all the way
Oh, what fun it is to ride
In a one-horse open sleigh, hey
Jingle bells, jingle bells
Jingle all the way
Oh, what fun it is to ride
In a one-horse open sleigh

A day or two ago
I thought I'd take a ride
And soon, Miss Fanny Bright
Was seated by my side
The horse was lean and lank
Misfortune seemed his lot
He got into a drifted bank
And then we got upsot

Joy To The World

A popular Christmas carol with lyrics by English writer
Isaac Watts based on Psalms 96, 98 and Genesis 3:17-18.
As of the late 20th century, "Joy to the World" was the
most-published Christmas hymn in North America.

Joy To The World

Joy to the world! The Lord is come
Let earth receive her King
Let ev'ry heart prepare Him room
And heav'n and nature sing
And heav'n and nature sing
And heav'n, and heav'n and nature sing

Joy to the world! The Savior reigns
Let men their songs employ
While fields and floods, rocks, hills and plains
Repeat the sounding joy
Repeat the sounding joy
Repeat, repeat the sounding joy

No more let sins and sorrows grow
Nor thorns infest the ground
He comes to make His blessings flow
Far as the curse is found
Far as the curse is found
Far as, far as the curse is found

He rules the world with truth and grace
And makes the nations prove
The glories of His righteousness
And wonders of His love, and wonders of His love
And wonders, and wonders of His love

O Christmas Tree

"O Christmas Tree" or "O Tannenbaum," a German Christmas carol, is based on a traditional folk song. Originally unrelated to Christmas, it became associated with the traditional Christmas tree in the middle of the 19th century.

O Christmas Tree

O Christmas Tree, O Christmas Tree,
How lovely are your branches.
O Christmas Tree, O Christmas Tree,
How lovely are your branches.
In beauty green will always grow,
Through summer sun and winter snow.
O Christmas Tree, O Christmas Tree,
How lovely are your branches.

O Christmas Tree, O Christmas Tree,
You give us so much pleasure!
O Christmas Tree, O Christmas Tree,
You give us so much pleasure!
How oft at Christmas tide the sight,
O green fir tree, gives us delight!
O Christmas Tree, O Christmas Tree,
You give us so much pleasure!

O Christmas Tree, O Christmas Tree,
How lovely are your branches.
O Christmas Tree, O Christmas Tree,
How lovely are your branches.
They're green when summer days are bright;
They're green when winter snow is white.
O Christmas Tree, O Christmas Tree,
How lovely are your branches.

O Come All Ye Faithful

Originally written in Latin as *Adeste Fideles*, this Christmas
carol has been attributed to various authors. The earliest
manuscript of the hymn is located in the library of the
Ducal Palace of Vila Viçosa. The original four verses
of the hymn were extended to eight, and
translated into many languages.

O Come All Ye Faithful

O come all ye faithful
Joyful and triumphant
O come ye, O come ye to Bethlehem
Come and behold Him
Born the King of angels

O come, let us adore Him
O come, let us adore Him
O come, let us adore Him
Christ the Lord

Sing, choirs of angels
Sing in exultation
O sing all ye bright hosts
Of heav'n above
Glory to God
All glory in the highest

Yea, Lord, we greet Thee
Born this happy morning
Jesus, to Thee be all glory giv'n
Word of the Father
Now in flesh appearing

O Come, O Come, Emmanuel

Originally written in Latin, "Veni, Veni, Emmanuel" as a hymn for Advent and Christmas. It was translated into English by John Mason Neale in 1851.

O Come, O Come, Emmanuel

O come, O come, Emmanuel,
And ransom captive Israel,
That mourns in lonely exile here
Until the Son of God appear.
Rejoice! Rejoice! Emmanuel
Shall come to thee, O Israel.

O come, Thou Rod of Jesse, free
Thine own from Satan's tyranny;
From depths of hell Thy people save,
And give them victory over the grave.
Rejoice! Rejoice! Emmanuel
Shall come to thee, O Israel.

O come, Thou Day-spring, come and cheer
Our spirits by Thine advent here;
And drive away the shades of night
And pierce the clouds and bring us light!
Rejoice! Rejoice! Emmanuel
Shall come to thee, O Israel.

O come, Thou Key of David, come,
And open wide our heavenly home;
Make safe the way that leads on high,
And close the path to misery.
Rejoice! Rejoice! Emmanuel
Shall come to thee, O Israel.

O Holy Night

A well-known Christmas carol composed by Adolphe Adam
in 1847 to the French poem "*Minuit, chrétiens*" (Midnight,
Christians) written by a wine merchant and poet,
Placide Cappeau (1808–1877). In both the French original
and the English version, the text reflects on the
birth of Jesus and on humanity's redemption.

O Holy Night

O holy night, the stars are brightly shining
It is the night of our dear Savior's birth
Long lay the world in sin and error pining
'Til He appeared and the soul felt its worth
A thrill of hope the weary world rejoices
For yonder breaks a new and glorious morn

Fall on your knees
O hear the angel voices
O night divine
O night when Christ was born
O night divine
O night, O night divine

Truly He taught us to love one another
His law is love and His gospel is peace
Chains shall He break, for the slave is our brother
And in His name all oppression shall cease
Sweet hymns of joy in grateful chorus raise we
Let all within me praise His holy name

Christ is the Lord!
Then ever, ever praise we
His power and glory, forevermore proclaim
His power and glory, forevermore proclaim

31

O Little Town Of Bethlehem

A popular Christmas carol written by Phillips Brooks
(1835–1893), an Episcopal priest, then rector of Church
of the Holy Trinity, Philadelphia. He was inspired by visiting
the village of Bethlehem in 1865 and wrote the poem for
his church three years later. The music was added by his
organist Lewis Redner (1831-1908).

O Little Town Of Bethlehem

O little town of Bethlehem
How still we see thee lie
Above thy deep and dreamless sleep
The silent stars go by
Yet in thy dark streets shineth
The everlasting Light
The hopes and fears of all the years
Are met in thee tonight

For Christ is born of Mary
And gathered all above
While mortals sleep
The angels keep their watch of wondering love
O morning stars together
Proclaim the holy birth
And praises sing to God the King
And peace to men on earth

O holy Child of Bethlehem
Descend to us we pray
Cast out our sin and enter in
Be born in us today
We hear the Christmas angels
The great glad tidings tell
O come to us, abide with us
Our Lord Emmanuel

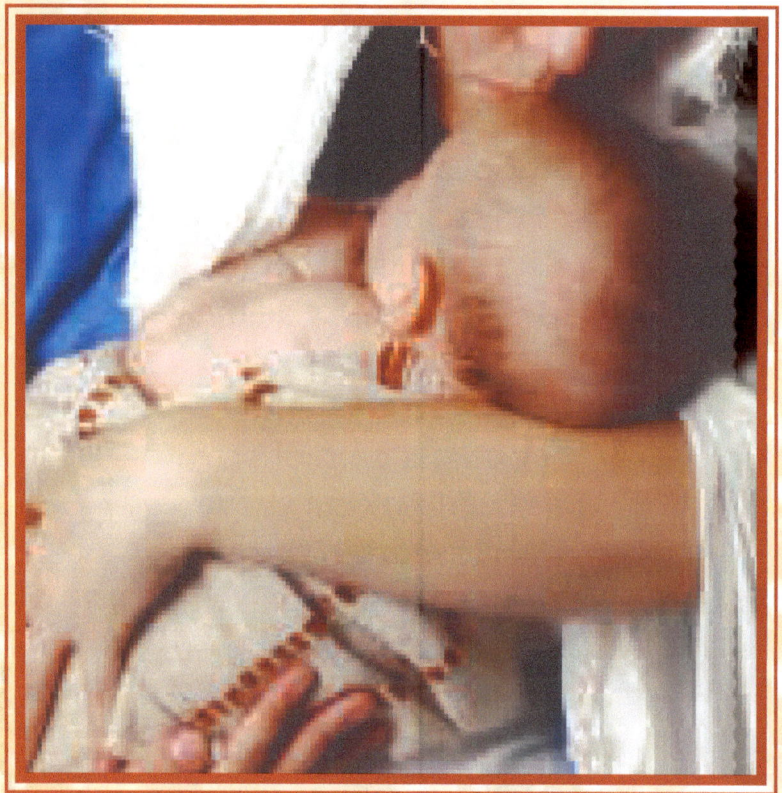

Silent Night

A popular Christmas carol, composed in 1818 by
Franz Xaver Gruber to lyrics by Joseph Mohr in the
small town of Oberndorf bei Salzburg, Austria. The song has
been recorded by a large number of singers from
every music genre. The version sung by Bing Crosby
is the third best-selling single of all time.

Silent Night

Silent night, holy night
All is calm, all is bright
'Round yon virgin mother and Child
Holy Infant so tender and mild
Sleep in heavenly peace
Sleep in heavenly peace

Silent night, holy night
Shepherds quake at the sight
Glories stream from heaven afar
Heavenly hosts sing alleluia
Christ, the Savior, is born
Christ, the Savior, is born

Silent night, holy night
Son of God, love's pure light
Radiant beams from Thy holy face
With the dawn of redeeming grace
Jesus, Lord, at Thy birth
Jesus, Lord, at Thy birth

The Twelve Days of Christmas

A Christian song written to celebrate the Nativity of Jesus.
and commemorate the twelve days from Christmas to
Epiphany as a sacred and festive season.

The Twelve Days of Christmas

On the first day of Christmas
My true love gave to me

A partridge in a pear tree

Second Day ~ Two turtle doves

Third Day ~ Three French hens

Fourth Day ~ Four calling birds

Fifth Day ~ Five golden rings

Sixth Day ~ Six geese a-laying

Seventh Day ~ Seven swans a-swimming

Eighth Day ~ Eight maids a-milking

Ninth Day ~ Nine ladies dancing

Tenth Day ~ Ten lords a-leaping

Eleventh Day ~ Eleven pipers piping

Twelfth Day ~ Twelve drummers drumming

37

We Three Kings

Written by John Henry Hopkins Jr. in 1857 for a Christmas pageant in New York City. Hopkins wrote this popular Christmas carol while serving as a rector of Christ Episcopal Church in Williamsport Pennsylvania.

We Three Kings

We three kings of Orient are;
Bearing gifts we traverse afar
Field and fountain, moor and mountain,
Following yonder star.

Chorus
O Star of wonder, star of night, Star with royal beauty bright,
Westward leading, still proceeding, Guide us to thy Perfect Light.

Born a King on Bethlehem's plain,
Gold I bring to crown Him again,
King forever, ceasing never
Over us all to reign. (Chorus)

Frankincense to offer have I;
Incense owns a Deity nigh;
Prayer and praising, all men raising,
Worship Him, God most high. (Chorus)

Myrrh is mine: its bitter perfume
Breathes of life of gathering gloom,
Sorrowing, sighing, bleeding, dying,
Sealed in the stone-cold tomb. (Chorus)

Glorious now behold Him arise, King and God and Sacrifice;
Alleluia, Alleluia! Earth to heav'n replies. (Chorus)

We Wish You A Merry Christmas

A popular English Christmas carol from the West Country of England. The composer, Arthur Warrell, is responsible for the popularity of the carol. Warrell arranged the tune for his own University of Bristol Madrigal Singers, who performed the carol in concert on December 6, 1935.

We Wish You A Merry Christmas

We wish you a merry Christmas
We wish you a merry Christmas
We wish you a merry Christmas
And a happy new year

Good tidings we bring to you and your friends
Good tidings for Christmas and a happy new year

What Child Is This?

Written by William Chatterton Dix in 1865. The lyrics were penned as a poem called "The Manger Throne" and subsequently set to the music of the traditional English folk song "Greensleeves."

What Child Is This?

What child is this, who, laid to rest,
On Mary's lap is sleeping,
Whom angels greet with anthems sweet
While shepherds watch are keeping?
This, this is Christ the King,
Whom shepherds guard and angels sing;
Haste, haste to bring Him laud,
The babe, the son of Mary!

Why lies He in such mean estate
Where ox and ass are feeding?
Good Christian, fear: for sinners here
The silent Word is pleading.
Nails, spear shall pierce him through,
The Cross be borne for me, for you;
Hail, hail the Word Made Flesh,
The babe, the son of Mary!

So bring Him incense, gold, and myrrh;
Come, peasant, king, to own Him!
The King of Kings salvation brings;
Let loving hearts enthrone Him!
Raise, raise the song on high!
The virgin sings her lullaby.
Joy! joy! for Christ is born,
The babe, the son of Mary!

CPSIA information can be obtained
at www.ICGtesting.com
Printed in the USA
BVHW020937091120
592840BV00003B/24